Gustav
HOLST
ST. PAUL'S SUITE
Orchestral Setting
H. 118B
Edited by
Clark McAlister

Study Score
Partitur

SERENISSIMA MUSIC, INC.

PREFACE

Gustav Holst neatly summarizes both the genesis and rationale of his *St. Paul's Suite* in a handwritten note which appears on the cover of his manuscript score:

This Suite was written for St Paul's Girls' school orchestra in 1912. By the time it was finished and copied the orchestra possessed wood wind instruments. Parts for the latter were added.

Gustav Holst
July 1922

Holst wrote the wind and timpani additions into his score in red ink. Most of these additions are very clear and are easily realized. In some places, however, such as mm.192-207 of the Viola line in the Jig, Holst simply says "all wind," apparently trusting the voicing of the wind chords to his copyist. Imogen Holst in *The Music of Gustav Holst* (Third Revised Edition) tells us that her father happily continued to add optional wind parts to this piece to accommodate students who wanted to play in the school orchestra, but in this edition I have confined myself to those wind parts actually written by Holst into his score.

The source score represents Holst's original version of the Suite, which is significantly different from the published version for string orchestra (Goodwin & Tabb, 1922). Among the more audible changes are these:

In the Ostinato there are four extra measures following measure 130 of the published version. The A-flats in mm.133-135 of the published version do not appear in the original score.

The published version of the Intermezzo (originally entitled Dance) is substantially shorter than the original by nearly seventy measures which follow measure 60.

The scoring of mm.193-210 of the Finale is quite different in the published version. The thematic material of this passage is the same in both versions, but the treatment in the published version is thicker and more vigorous. The original version, by comparison, is lean and simple.

Since the score used to engrave the published version has been lost, and since none of the composer's published correspondence refer to these matters, we can only theorize about Holst's reasons for making these changes for publication. Holst conceived his wind parts in terms of this score, and performed the suite in this way. For the above reason, this edition of the "orchestral" version of the *St. Paul's Suite* follows Holst's manuscript score and retains, among other differences, the extended movements and scoring variants described above.

Clark McAlister

ORCHESTRA

2 Flutes

Oboe

2 Clarinets (A, B-flat)

Horn (F)

Timpani

Violin I

Violin II

Viola

Violoncello

Double Bass

Duration: ca.13 minutes
Composed 1913, wind parts added ca.1920.

ISMN: 979-0-58042-746-5

© Copyright 2005 by Clark McAlister.
Engraved by Giuliano Forghieri.

St. Paul's Suite

I. Jig

GUSTAV HOLST, H. 118b
Arranged by the Composer
Edited by Clark McAlister

Copyright ©2005 Clark McAlister.
42172

II. Ostinato

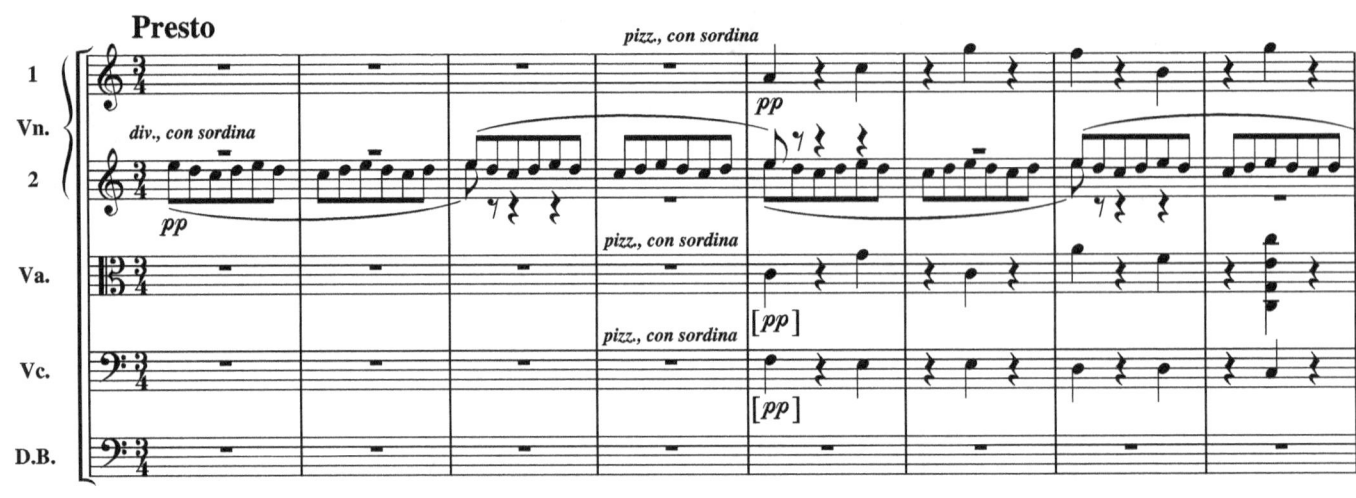
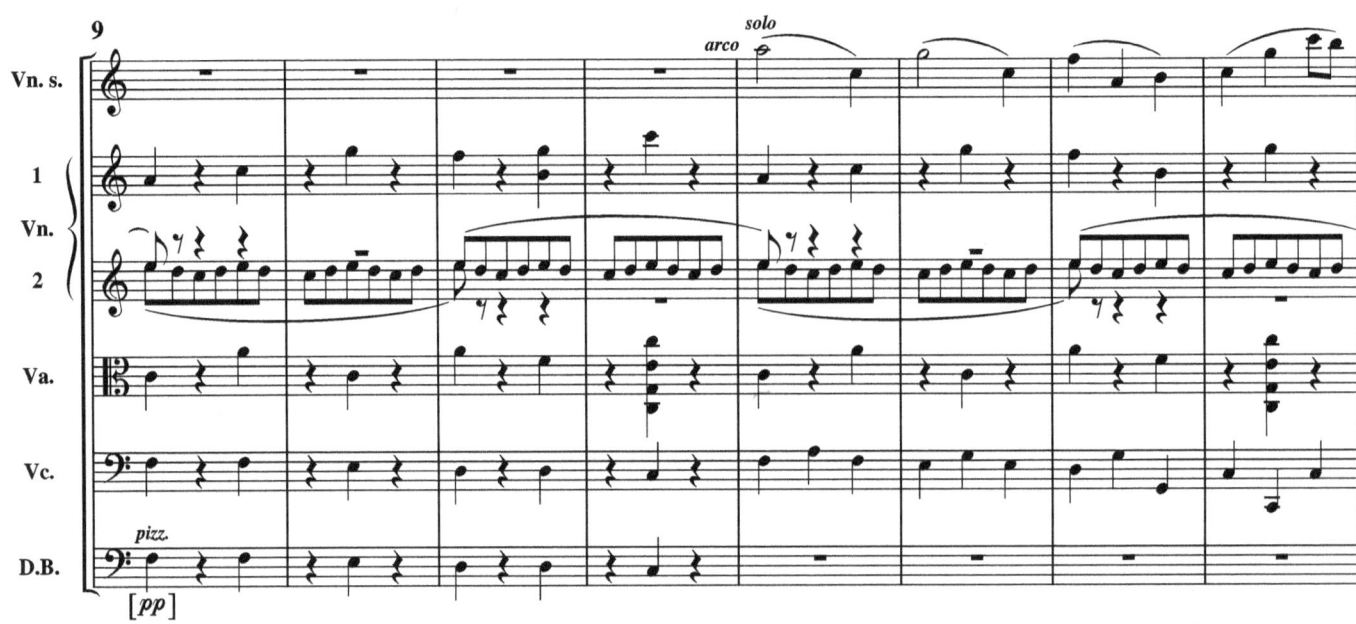
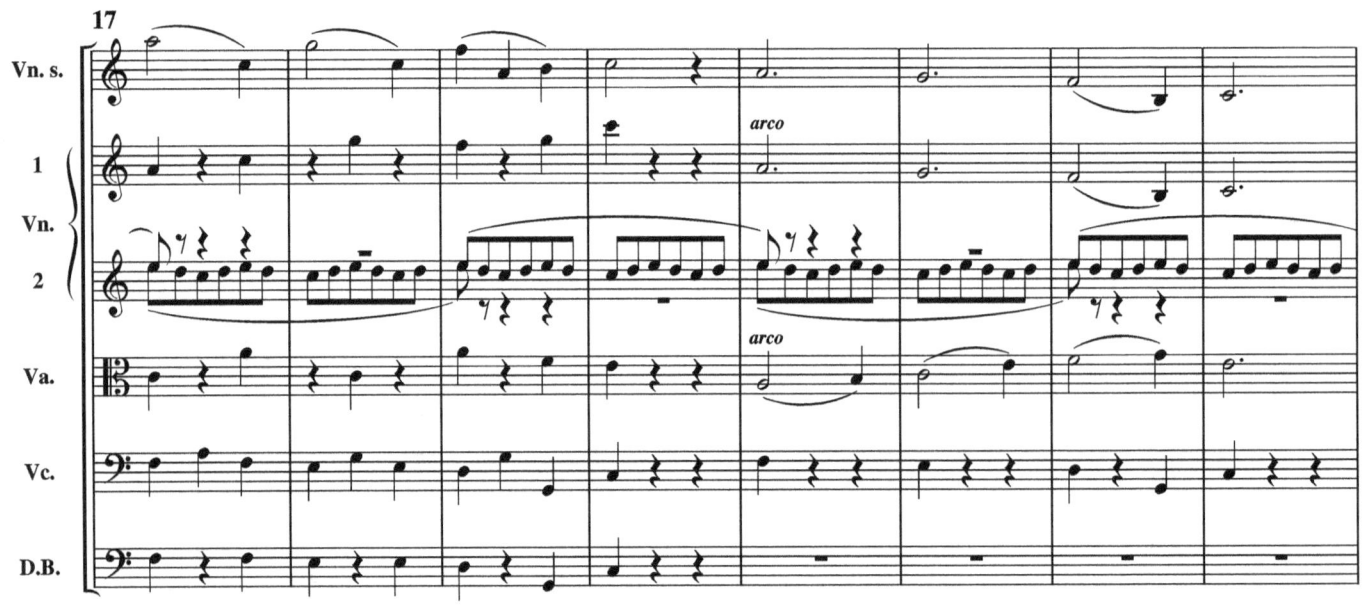

* Violoncello, m. 37--Neither Holst's score nor the published score or parts show this arco, but the music clearly requires it.

21

III. Dance

NB--In the published string orchestra version, this title has been changed to **Intermezzo**.

26

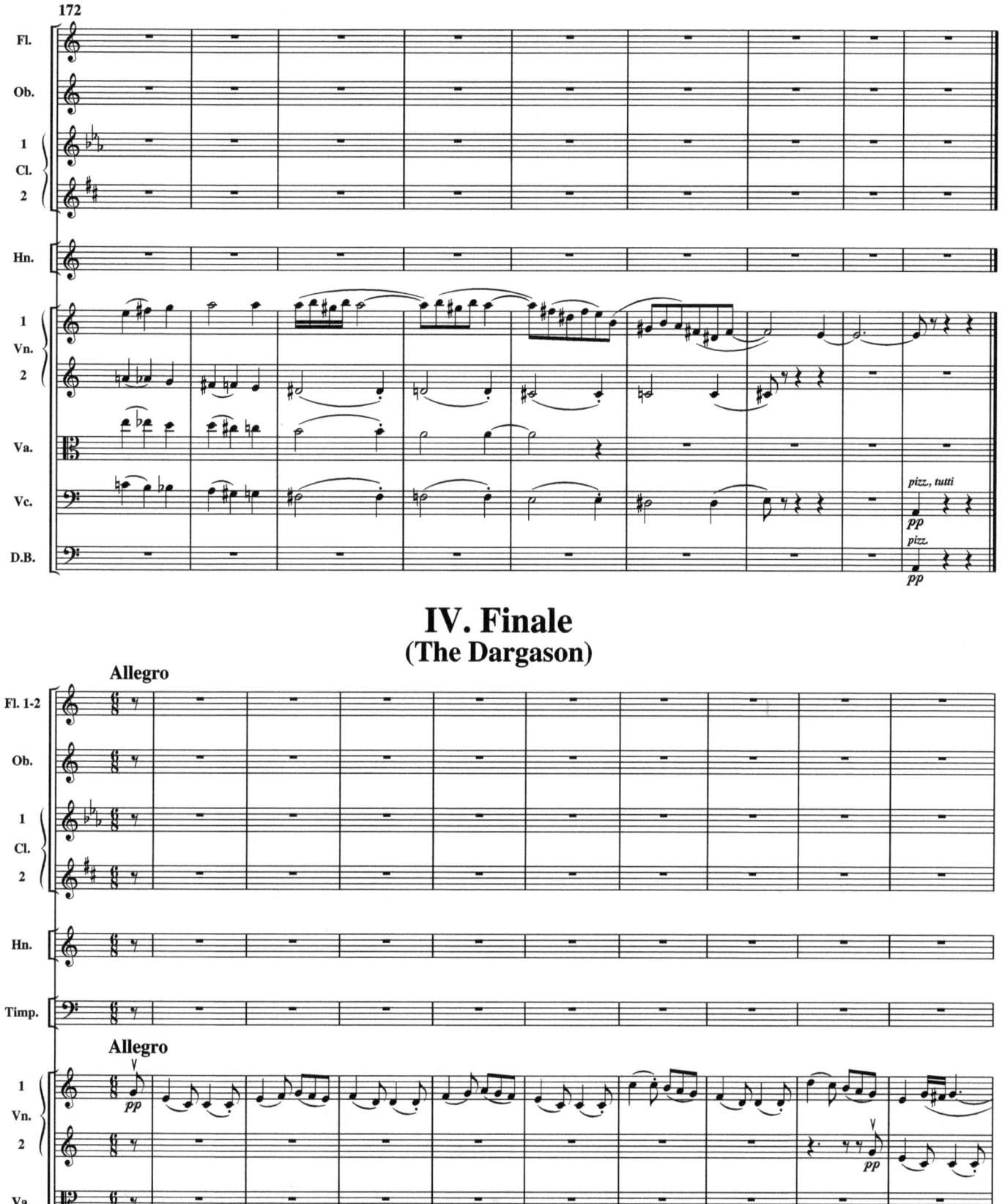

IV. Finale
(The Dargason)

34

37

www.ingramcontent.com/pod-product-compliance
Lightning Source LLC
Chambersburg PA
CBHW081351040426
42450CB00015B/3393